PENGUIN

THE END OF INDIA

Khushwant Singh was born in 1915 in Hadali, Punjab. He was educated at Government College, Lahore and at King's College and the Inner Temple in London. He practised at the Lahore High Court for several years before joining the Indian Ministry of External Affairs in 1947. He was sent on diplomatic postings to Canada and London and later went to Paris with UNESCO. He began a distinguished career as a journalist with All India Radio in 1951. Since then he has been founder-editor of *Yojana*, and editor of *The Illustrated Weekly of India*, *National Herald* and *Hindustan Times*. Today he is India's best-known columnist and journalist.

Khushwant Singh has also had an extremely successful career as a writer. Among his published works are the classic two-volume *History of the Sikhs*, several works of fiction including the novels *Train to Pakistan* (winner of the Grove Press Award for the best work of fiction in 1954), *I Shall Not Hear the Nightingale*, *Delhi* and *The Company of Women* and a number of translated works and non-fiction books on Delhi, nature and current affairs.

Khushwant Singh was a member of Parliament from 1980 to 1986. Among other honours, he was awarded the Padma Bhushan in 1974 by the President of India (he returned the decoration in 1984 in protest against the Union Government's siege of the Golden Temple, Amritsar). His autobiography, *Truth, Love and a Little Malice*, was published in 2002.

THE END OF INDIA

Khushwant Singh

PENGUIN BOOKS

Penguin Books India (P) Ltd., 11 Community Centre,
Panchsheel Park, New Delhi 110 017, India
Penguin Books Ltd., 80 Strand, London WC2R 0RL, UK
Penguin Putnam Inc., 375 Hudson Street, New York,
NY 10014, USA
Penguin Books Australia Ltd., 250 Camberwell Road,
Camberwell, Victoria 3124, Australia
Penguin Books Canada Ltd., 10 Alcorn Avenue, Suite 300,
Toronto, Ontario, M4V 3B2, Canada
Penguin Books (NZ) Ltd., Cnr Rosedale and Airborne Roads,
Albany, Auckland, New Zealand
Penguin Books (South Africa) (Pty) Ltd.,
24 Sturdee Avenue, Rosebank 2196, South Africa

First published by Penguin Books India 2003

Copyright © Khushwant Singh 2003

Some of the material used in these essays first appeared in
The Illustrated Weekly of India and in *Hindustan Times*.

All rights reserved

10 9 8 7 6 5 4 3 2 1

Typeset in *Times New Roman* by SÜRYA, New Delhi
Printed at Chaman Offset Printers, New Delhi

To all those who love India

CONTENTS

Introduction   1

The Case of Gujarat   23

The Sangh and Its Demons   39

Communalism—An Old Problem   75

Is There a Solution?   125

INTRODUCTION

These are dark times for India. The carnage in Gujarat, Bapu Gandhi's home state, in early 2002 and the subsequent landslide victory of Narendra Modi in the elections will spell disaster for our country. The fascist agenda of Hindu fanatics is unlike anything we have experienced in our modern history. After Partition I had thought we would never again experience a similar holocaust. I may be proved wrong. Far from becoming mahaan (great), India is going to the dogs, and unless a miracle saves us, the country will break up. It will not be Pakistan or any other foreign power that will destroy us; we will commit hara-kiri.

At the time India won its independence in 1947, most India-watchers did not foresee this danger. Their concern was the left. They predicted that within a few years communists would take over the country. Marxist pedagogues assured everyone who cared to listen to them that India was like a rotten apple hanging on the branch of a rootless tree that could fall with the slightest tremor of the earth. There were enormous disparities between the few very rich and privileged on the one side and the teeming millions of the impoverished, underprivileged and discriminated against on the other. It was only a matter of time before the peasants and workers would rise en masse and sweep the bourgeoisie into the sea.

There were good reasons to believe that this would be the shape of things to come. Between 1939 and 1945, the years of the Second World War, while Congress leaders were behind bars for not co-operating with the government, communists who supported the British and their allies against fascists were allowed to consolidate their strength. They came to dominate workers trade unions across the country; they set up kisan organizations committed to depriving landlords of excess land. In every university they had Marxist students unions; they had progressive writers unions, people's theatre groups and bodies like Friends of the Soviet Union. They had infiltrated the army, navy and police. They were confident that no sooner the war ended and the British packed up to leave, they would take over the country.

All their calculations went awry because they had grossly misread the mood of the people. As soon as the war was over and Congress leaders set free, people condemned communists as collaborators of the hated British. Their new heroes were Netaji Subhash Chandra Bose and others of the now defunct Indian National Army which had fought on the side of the Japanese against the British. The communists had also underestimated the hold of Mahatma Gandhi on the Indian masses; the Mahatma had no compassion for Godless Marxists. Above all, it was Jawaharlal Nehru, India's first prime minister, who took the wind out of the communists' sails by making India a socialist country. The strength the communists had gathered withered away. I recall Kingsley Martin, editor of the left-wing *New Statesman* and *Nation* and a friend of Nehru's, telling me on one of his visits to India, 'My dear fellow, how can you take Indian communists seriously? They play cricket matches against teams of anti-communists!'

All this while a new threat was growing, slowly but surely. Nehru was the first and probably the only leader of the time who sensed that the challenge to India's democracy would come not from communism but from a resurgence of religious fanaticism. He had spent the best part of his nine years in jail studying Indian and world history. He knew that every organized religion harkened back to an imagined glorious past and opposed change. In Europe, secular forces had to wage battles with the church and compel it to restrict its activities to matters spiritual. This did not happen in the Islamic world. As a consequence, Muslim nations remained backward and largely undemocratic. What would become of predominantly Hindu India, now that it was truly independent for the first time in centuries? Indian democracy was fragile, and unless it struck strong secular roots, it would crumble and fall. India had religious minorities like Muslims (12%), Christians (3%) and Sikhs (2%). Muslims and Christians were scattered across the country and not likely to create problems. Sikhs were concentrated in the Punjab but were too small in numbers, too closely related to the Hindus and therefore manageable. The main danger to India's secular democracy would be the resurgence of religious fundamentalism among Hindus who formed over 80% of the population. Nehru was able to fight it off as long as he lived. It might be recalled that when Dr Rajendra Prasad agreed to inaugurate the newly rebuilt temple at Somnath, Nehru sent a strong note protesting that the President of a secular State had no business to involve himself in religious matters. Unfortunately, the leaders who came after Nehru were not as upright and staunchly secular. Hindu extremist groups began to grow in strength.

The feeling that Hindus had been deprived of their legacy and humiliated by foreigners had deep roots. For eight centuries, Muslim dynasties had ruled over the country, and many Muslim rulers had destroyed Hindu temples, made forcible conversions and imposed jazia (discriminatory taxes) on their non-Muslim subjects. This was not peculiar to the Muslim rulers of India. In almost all ancient and medieval societies this was the norm. Hindu rulers too, for instance, had persecuted Buddhists and Jains and destroyed their places of worship. The British, who followed the Mughals, tried to be even-handed in their dealings with Hindus and Muslims, but allowed Christian missionaries to open a vast network of schools, colleges and hospitals, preach the gospel of Christ and win converts to their faith.

It was during British rule that Hindu nationalism took birth. The most powerful movement, the Arya Samaj, began under the leadership of Swami Dayanand Saraswati (1824-1883). His call 'Back to the Vedas' received wide response, particularly in northern India. Amongst the Arya Samaj converts was the Punjabi Lala Lajpat Rai (1865-1928) who was both an ardent Hindu and a leader of the Indian National Congress. So was Bal Gangadhar Tilak (1856-1920) of Maharashtra who revived the cult of Ganapati and coined the slogan 'Swaraj is our birthright'. In due course of time, Hindu militant organizations took birth. The most important of these was the Rashtriya Swayamsevak Sangh (RSS) founded in 1925 by Keshav Baliram Hedgewar (1889-1940) in Nagpur. He propagated the cause of a Hindu rashtra, a Hindu state. He was anti-Muslim and also anti-Gandhi, because the Mahatma strove for equal rights for all religions. Hedgewar was succeeded by M.S. Golwalkar, who was followed by Balasaheb Deoras. Together, these leaders, all charismatic and all unashamedly communal, strengthened the organization through fascist propaganda, strict discipline and targeted social work among the Hindus during calamities like earthquakes and famines and during Partition.

By 1990, the RSS had over one million members, who included, among others, Atal Behari Vajpayee, L.K. Advani, Murli Manohar Joshi, Uma Bharti—the last three charged with the destruction of the Babri Masjid on 6 December 1992—and Narendra Modi, the present poster boy of the Hindu right who presided over the pogrom in Gujarat. The RSS was, and is, anti-Muslim, anti-Christian and anti-left. It could be dismissed as a lunatic group as long as it remained on the fringes of mainstream politics. Not any more. Its political offshoot, the Bharatiya Jan Sangh, today's Bharatiya Janata Party, had only two MPs in the Lok Sabha in 1984, but by 1991 it had 117. Today, with its allies, it rules the country.

There are now several other Hindu organizations as, if not more, militant than the RSS. There is the Shiv Sena led by the rabble-rouser Bal Thackerey, an admirer of Adolf Hitler. He started with a movement called 'Maharashtra for Maharashtrians' aimed at ousting South Indians from Bombay. His mission soon changed to ousting Muslims from India. In the last decade or so he has spread his tentacles across the country and boasts of his sainiks taking the leading part in destroying the mosque in Ayodhya. Perhaps as reward he has his quota of ministers in the central government. Besides the Shiv Sena, there are the more mischievous Bajrang Dal and the Vishva Hindu Parishad, currently leading the agitation to build a Ramjanmabhoomi temple on the exact site where the now-destroyed Babri Masjid stood—no matter what the government or the courts of law have to say. This is typical. Most members of the extended Sangh parivar regard themselves above the law of the land. They have arrogated to themselves the right to decide the fate of one billion Indians.

*

We Indians have always been more concerned about the race, religion and caste we were born into than about our being Indian nationals. Ever since the BJP and its allies came to power, a sinister dimension has been added to this feeling of separateness. It is hard to believe that elements of the Sangh parivar have been able to convince a significant number of Hindus that they have been treated as second-class citizens in a country where they form eighty-two per cent of the population. Whence this inferiority complex? How have the likes of Narendra Modi, Praveen Togadia, Ashok Singhal and Giriraj Kishore succeeded in persuading the Hindus that they are discriminated against when there is no evidence whatsoever to substantiate their claims?

The juggernaut of Hindu fundamentalism has emerged from the temple of intolerance and is on its yatra. Whoever stands in its way will be crushed under its mighty wheels. We used to boast with rightful pride that Hinduism was the most accommodating of all religions and India, which is predominantly Hindu, among the most tolerant of nations in its treatment of minorities. Hindu savants like Swami Vivekananda, Sri Aurobindo, Jiddu Krishnamurti, Swami Prabhupada, Osho and the sadhus of the Ramakrishna Mission took the message of Hinduism abroad, built temples and made many converts to Hinduism. Adherents of both Christianity and Islam, which have the largest and second largest following in the world respectively, conceded that Hinduism was unique in allowing that there were different ways of getting to the Truth of existence and everyone had the right to approach God in his or her own way. It laid no claim to monopoly over spiritual matters and was free of dogma and bigotry. In recent years, this image has taken a beating. Discrimination against Muslims culminating in the demolition of the Babri Masjid and then the massacres in Gujarat by Hindu terrorists destroyed the notion that Hinduism is more tolerant than Islam. The murder of Christian missionaries, attacks on churches and schools and the burning of Bibles have done similar damage to the perception of Hinduism among Christians.

The worst enemy of every religion is the fanatic who professes to follow it and tries to impose his view of his faith on others. People do not judge religions by what their prophets preached or how they lived but by the way their followers practice them. Christianity has a hard time explaining its inquisitors. Muslims will continue to be judged by the acts of groups like the Taliban and the Mujahideens who wage unending wars against the non-Muslims. And now Hinduism will be judged by the utterances of people like Uma Bharti, Sadhvi Rithambara and Praveen Togadia and the doings of Dara Singh, Narendra Modi and Bal Thackeray.

Fascism has well and truly crossed our threshold and dug its heels in our courtyard. And we have only ourselves to blame for this. We let the fanatics get away with every step they took without raising a howl of protest. They burnt books they did not like; they beat up journalists who wrote against them; they attacked cinema houses showing films they did not approve of; they smashed the equipment of film-makers ready to shoot film scripts cleared by the government; they vandalized the studio and paintings of India's leading artist (not surprisingly, a Muslim); they perverted texts from history books to make them conform to their ideas. We allowed them to do all this, as if none of this was our business. Now they openly butcher people for the crime of believing in a different God. They foul-mouth everyone who disagrees with them. To them we are pseudo-secularists. We failed to hit back because we were not a united force and did not realize the perils of allowing our country to fall into their hands. Now we are paying the price.

In her novel *In Times of Siege*, Githa Hariharan quotes a German Pastor, Reverend Martin Niemöller, who was persecuted by the Nazis:

'In Germany, they first came for the communists, and I did not speak up because I was not a communist. Then they came for the Jews, and I did not speak up because I was not a Jew.

'Then they came for the trade unionists, and I did not speak up because I was not a trade unionist.

'Then they came for the homosexuals, and I did not speak up because I was not a homosexual.

'Then they came for the Catholics, and I did not speak up because I was Protestant.

'Then they came for me . . . but by that time there was no one left to speak up.'

In my defence I can say with a clean conscience that I did raise my voice against religious fundamentalism and fanaticism whenever it surfaced. I condemned Jarnail Singh Bhindranwale when he made hateful utterances against Hindus. I was on his hit list and that of the Khalistanis and had to be guarded for fifteen years. Disillusioned with the Congress, I had proposed the name of L.K. Advani as MP from New Delhi in 1989, but have never spared him after he launched his notorious rath yatra from Somnath to Ayodhya. Once I confronted him at an open public meeting and told him to his face, 'You sowed the dragon seeds of hatred in this country which led to the breaking of the Babri Masjid.' Now in response to my columns I get hate mail from Hindu fundamentalists. Not a week goes by without my receiving a letter or postcard describing me as a disgrace to Sikhism and India, or a Pakistani agent—'Pakistani randi ki aulad (born of a Pakistani whore)'. And much more that is unprintably obscene. It washes over me like water on a duck's back. I have not given up nor will I give up because I feel I owe it to my country to fight these forces of evil for as long as I can.

Enough of heroics. I am not cast in a hero's mould. I am a coward, but I do speak my mind when it comes to real enemies of my country. That is the least I can do. For a long time I was searching for an appropriate word to describe religious fundamentalists. At last I have found it in Githa Hariharan's novella. She calls them 'fundoos' and defines them perfectly:

> 'A nickname, *fundoos*, rolls off Meena's tongue with ease. A nickname for a pet, a pet enemy. The familiar garden-variety hatemonger,

inescapable because he has taken root in your own backyard. Fundoo, fundamentalist. Fascist. Obscurantist. Terrorist. And the made-in-India brand, the communalist—a deceptively innocuous-sounding name for professional other-community haters.'

The essays in this book were written in anguish, anger and bouts of depression when I felt that we had lost the battle against the 'fundoos'. We have lost in Gujarat, we may lose in some other states and the 'fundoos' may rule over us while paying lip service to secularism—or not even that. But I still hope that revulsion against them will build up and they will eventually be thrown into the garbage can of history, where they belong. It is the duty of every sane Indian to put them there.

February 2003

THE CASE OF GUJARAT

There are days when speeches made by our netas and so-called sants distress me so much that a voice within me screams, 'Let all of them go to jahannum (hell). I'll get on with my life as best as I can.' When I get over the depression, a wave of anger surges within me and I say to myself: 'This is my homeland, I will not let these medieval-minded fanatics get away with wasting precious years squabbling over where exactly a temple should have its foundation-stone laid. I will shout my protest from the roof-tops.'

Then comes the ghastly carnage in Gujarat.

Much has been written and said about the riots of 2002. But not enough. I would like to quote from a document from another time. Summing up his report for the Maharashtra government after the riots in Bhiwandi and Jalgaon in 1970, Judge Madon wrote:

'It was a lonely, arduous and weary journey through a land of hatred and violence, of prejudice and perjury. The encounters on the way were with men without compassion, lusting for the blood of their fellow men, with politicians who trafficked in communal hatred and religious fanaticism, with local leaders who sought power by sowing disunity and bitterness, with police officers and policemen who

were unworthy of their uniform, with
investigating officers without honour
and without scruples, with men
committed to falsehood and wedded
to fraud and with dealers in mayhem
and murder.'

He could have been writing about Narendra
Modi's Gujarat. But at least the Maharashtra
government under S.B. Chavan accepted Judge
Madon's damning report with all its
recommendations. Modi's government
dismissed the report of the National Human
Rights Commission as incorrect and biased.
The Central government's attitude was no
different. Cabinet ministers like Arun Jaitley
shamelessly supported Modi's stand. To them
it was mere propaganda by the 'pseudo-
secularists'.

What can one expect from an administration that has openly sided with murderers? It is clear that the attack on the train at Godhra was pre-planned. Far from putting the perpetrators down with an iron hand, the government colluded with the mischief-makers as its police and its chief minister were imbued with the spirit of badla—revenge. It is also clear that the revenge was so vicious and effective because it was also pre-planned. There have been credible reports that within hours of the Godhra massacre, armed mobs were out in different parts of Gujarat with detailed lists of Muslim homes and establishments. Several hundred Muslims were hacked to death or burnt alive, women raped, homes and shops looted and burnt down.

I have seen it before with my own eyes in 1947 and 1984. The police stood by like tamashbeens (spectators) watching the carnage. They had been tipped off not to interfere but let looters and killers teach hapless men, women and children a lesson they would never forget.

In Gujarat they went several steps further. Not only did the police remain inert, when the army arrived on the scene, it was not deployed. Flag marches are spectacles which don't frighten evil-doers. What does frighten them are orders to shoot at sight which were issued too late, only after many lives had been lost. Officers who tried to do their duty and foil the plans of the mobs were transferred out. Even in the camps set up for the riot victims there was harassment.

There can be no doubt there was serious dereliction of duty on the part of the chief minister, his cabinet colleagues and the IG of police. Even a year after the rioting, many Muslim victims remain homeless. Those who have returned to their homes have been forced to withdraw all complaints filed with the police. They are at the mercy of their Hindu neighbours who have warned them never to forget their subordinate status. I won't be surprised if Muslims in Gujarat one day have to start paying religious taxes like the jazia which medieval Islamic rulers imposed on their non-Muslim subjects.

*

It is ironic that the highest incidence of violence against Muslims and Christians has taken place in Gujarat, the home state of Bapu Gandhi. It has been going on for years. Before the 2002 riots, Christian missionaries were being attacked in the tribal districts of the state. There were reports of violence and intimidation coming in almost every day. We will see more of that.

Since the late 1990s, newspaper reports have put the blame for this communalization squarely on neo-fascist members of the Sangh parivar: the RSS, Vishwa Hindu Parishad, Bajrang Dal and Shiv Sena, with the collusion of the BJP government. Reports of the Minorities Commission substantiate what has appeared in the national press. For those interested, photographic evidence of destroyed churches, dargahs, Muslim homes and shops is available. Among the most ludicrous is the State-sponsored attempt to wipe out remnants of Muslim presence. I first saw this in 1998. Gujarat's capital, Ahmedabad, was built by a Muslim ruler in the middle ages. I noticed that milestones on the main highway leading to the city had dropped Ahmed from its name and made it into Amdavad.

How did Gujarat become the laboratory of Hindutva? It did not happen overnight. The Sangh and its sympathizers began poisoning Gujarat not long after Independence. Even the Congress took advantage of the slowly vitiating atmosphere to divide Gujarati society for electoral gains, unwittingly helping the RSS. The 1969 Ahmedabad riots were the first triumph of the RSS in Gujarat. Its fortunes began rising after that.

I went to Ahmedabad in 1970, five months after the riots. I quote from the article I wrote after my return:

'I had constituted myself into a one-man commission of enquiry to find out all I could in three days and pass on my verdict to my readers. My object was not to discover what had happened . . . but why it happened.

And, even more, what the people of Ahmedabad thought about it today and what they would do tomorrow if some incident again strained relations between the city's 90% Hindus and 10% Muslims.

'I start my investigation by visiting the temple of Jagannath . . . I detect no signs of damage. To make sure I ask (a) priest. He tells me to look outside. I go outside and look. Above the entrance gate is a glass pane to cover an effigy of a mahant. The pane is splintered in three places. I approach a band of ash-smeared sadhus lolling under the shade of a banyan tree and ask them if anything else had been damaged . . . They express themselves in unholy language.

'I walk around the bazaar and come to the dargah where it is said to have begun—with the herd of temple cows stampeding into pilgrims going to some Urs. The dargah gate is barred. A posse of constabulary guard the entrance. I ask the caretaker seated outside if this is the right place. He looks at me suspiciously. For an answer he spits a blob of phlegm on the pavement. The sub-inspector of police gives me a dirty look. I do not like policemen. I move on.

'I go to the Sindhi Bazaar. It is a cluster of cubicles made of plywood and corrugated tin. Row upon row of mini-shops cluttered with bales of cloth and hung with multicoloured saris. The place looks as inflammable as an Indian Oil petrol carrier. I was told that the bazaar had gone up in smoke. I can well believe it. But I see no sign of damage. Sindhis are an enterprising race; they must have rebuilt it and resumed business. I accept one of the many invitations hurled at me to buy something . . . I pay for a dhoti to buy information. I get an earful of hate.

'I hire a scooter. From the Arabic numerals 786 painted on the metre I know the faith of the driver. A scooter is not the best mode of transport for a friendly dialogue. I yell my comment on the 'bad days'. The driver turns back, 'You take me for a sucker? I know on which side you are!' He doesn't say so with his tongue but with his doleful eyes.

'I try paanwalas, chanawalas, fruit vendors. The result is the same. If they talk, they are Hindus. If they do not, they are Muslims. Both speech and silence are pregnant with hate . . .

'I remind myself of my mission. It is not to probe into the dead past but to gauge the prevailing mood and so forecast the future. But the yesterdays of September are always with me. I drive out of Ahmedabad along the Sabarmati. I pass a mound of debris. A half-broken minaret reveals its identity. I pass graves with their gravestones smashed. And my temper mounts and tears come to my eyes. What species of monstrous swine were those who spared neither places of worship nor the peace of the dead?'

At the end of my visit I told the then Mayor of Ahmedabad about what I had seen and heard. 'It is all over,' he assured me. 'It will not happen again.' I hoped he was right. But I was not so sure.

Of course it did happen again, more than once, and most tragically in February 2002. Those deep divisions I saw over thirty years ago were not allowed to heal. The Sanghwalas were never interested in bringing communities together. In Gujarat, a border state, they have terrorized and alienated the state's ten per cent Muslim population. History will judge them for the damage they have caused, but that will happen in the future. Meanwhile, with a triumphant Modi as their mentor, they will repeat the Gujarat experiment all over India, unless we stop them.

THE SANGH AND ITS DEMONS

All religions have and continue to have bigots who give founders of their religion and their teachings a bad name. Christians had their inquisitors who burnt innocent men and women at the stake as heretics. Muslims have their Islamic fraternities whose leaders pronounce fatwas condemning people to death, ordering women to shroud themselves in veils and imposing draconian rules of behaviour on the community. Sikhs had their Bhindranwale who forbade men to dye or roll up their beards, women to wear saris or jeans or put bindis on their foreheads, and who said nasty things about dhotian-topian waaley—the Hindus. Not to be outdone, Hindus produced their own fanatics who condemn Christianity and Islam as alien religions, and while mouthing platitudes about being the most tolerant religion on earth, hound Christian missionaries and target Muslim places of worship for destruction. In the name of Shri Rama, they demolished the Babri Masjid in Ayodhya, and Gujarat represented the worst face of religious extremism.

Events such as the demolition of the Babri masjid, the burning of Graham Staines and his children and the barbaric and mindless carnage in Gujarat stink of politics mixed with religion. I have always maintained that religion and politics do not go together; they must be kept apart at all cost. But the Hinduization of Indian politics, the sporulation of Hindu-chauvinistic parties, and the rise of the BJP to centre stage all point to an alarming and disturbing truth: religio-centric politics is here to stay and its evils will be more enduring and damaging than you or I can imagine.

The birth of Hindu nationalism took place in Renaissance Bengal in 1886 with the Hindu melas. The primary objective of these melas was to train young Hindus in the martial arts, the use of lathis, daggers and swords. Non-Hindus were not allowed to participate. There was Swami Dayanand Saraswati's Arya Samaj movement with its emphasis on Shuddhi—Dayanand's objective to re-establish the golden age of Hinduism encouraged reconversion of Muslims and Christians back to its fold. In Maharashtra, Bal Gangadhar Tilak revived Ganapati and Shivaji festivals. Every time they were celebrated, Hindu-Muslim riots broke out. At the same time, in Bengal, anusilan samitis (disciplinary organizations) were set up to combat partition of the state. These samitis did not accept non-Hindus as members. Hindu Sabhas, which had initially stood for cow protection, the promotion of Hindi as a national language, and self-rule, formally launched the Hindu Mahasabha in 1922. But it was only after the arrival of V.D. Savarkar as its president in 1936 that the organization assumed a distinctive Hindu ideology, a theory of a Hindu nation. At the core of this ideology was Savarkar's *Hindutva*, published in 1923.

According to Savarkar, a Hindu is one who acknowledges Hindustan as his pitrubhumi (fatherland) as well as his punyabhumi (holy land). Whether he or she is a devotee of sanatan dharma is unimportant. Anyone who is or whose ancestor was Hindu in undivided India—including someone who was originally a Hindu but converted to Islam or Christianity—is also welcome back into the Hindu fold provided he accepts India as his fatherland and land of worship. However, love for Bharat Mata, following the Hindu faith and belief in the Hindu caste system are not enough. A Hindu has to love, embrace—and own—Hindu sanskriti as a whole. This automatically excluded Muslims and Christians, for, while they might have shared a common pitrubhumi with the Hindus, their punyabhumi lay elsewhere. Hindutva also involved the wholehearted acceptance of Sanskrit and other Indian languages while there was no place for Urdu or English. While Jains, Buddhists and Sikhs were accepted because their religions were of Indian origin, Muslims, Christians and

Parsis were excluded on the basis that they were 'communities of numerical minorities'.

Savarkar was also the first to propound the two-nation theory, referring to the Hindus and Muslims as separate nations. Other Hindu leaders who accepted this two-nation theory were Dr Moonje of the Hindu Mahasabha, Pandit Madan Mohan Malaviya, founder of the Benaras Hindu University, Lala Lajpat Rai, Bhai Parmanand and Swami Shraddhanand. The eminent Bengali writer Bankimchandra Chattopadhyay also supported the notion.

The stream of Hindu separatism began to flow like the Pataal Ganga soon after the British overthrew the Mughal dynasty and established their rule all over India. It gathered strength from reviving and exaggerating memories—

real and imaginary—of all the 'wrongs' the Muslim invaders had done in India: humiliating Hindu rulers on battlefields, destroying Hindu temples, imposing the jazia tax and treating non-Muslims as lower than second-class citizens. Hindu and Sikh warriors like Prithviraj Chauhan, Guru Gobind Singh and Shivaji who resisted the Muslim rulers, were portrayed as national heroes.

A general feeling was created that the wrongs done by Muslim conquerors in the past had to be set right. The Indian Freedom Movement was biased against the British as it was against Muslims. By the time the British decided to quit India, a significant proportion of Hindus felt that they should inherit the legacy of their forefathers while the vast majority of Indian Muslims felt that they would have no future in Hindu-dominated India. The inevitable partition of the country into India and Pakistan followed.

India could have declared itself a Hindu State since over eighty per cent of its population was Hindu and all its neighbours had declared themselves religious States: Islamic (Pakistan), Buddhist (Sri Lanka and Burma) and Hindu (Nepal). But under the influence of Gandhi, Nehru, Azad and others, it chose to pursue a greater ideal: a modern secular State where all religious communities would enjoy equal rights.

It was too good to last. What in Nehru's time were parties of marginal importance, the RSS, the Hindu Mahasabha, the Jan Sangh, the Shiv Sena and the Bajrang Dal, gathered strength and became the main opposition to secular forces. Drawing inspiration from Savarkar's concept of Hindutva, which they considered as an article of faith, they indulged in falsifying history, mosque-breaking, church-burning and attacking missionaries, and they went on to perpetrate pogroms. They are the footsoldiers of today's rulers. But if India is to survive as a nation and march forward, it must remain one country, reassert its secular credentials and throw out communally-based parties from the political arena.

A country which is proud of its tradition of religious tolerance and is the world's largest democracy has to reckon with forces that threaten to wreck both our past and present as well as demolish our dreams of the future. These forces can be easily identified as the lunatic fringe of the Sangh parivar—the Shiv Sena, the VHP, the Bajrang Dal, and a crop of new organizations raising suicide squads. No State worth its name should allow private armies to operate on its soil.

Ex-MP and former editor of the weekly *BJP Today*, Praful Goradia, like the leaders of the RSS (from Hedgewar and Golwalkar to the ones today), the Shiv Sena's Bal Thakeray, leaders of the VHP, Bajrang Dal and others of the Sangh parivar (including the BJP), believes in Savarkar's Hindutva. An ardent admirer of the Nehru-Gandhi family not so long ago, and an aspirant for a Congress ticket during Rajiv Gandhi's tenure, Goradia is the author of a booklet, *Thus Spoke Indira Gandhi*. Notwithstanding his past, he is a neo-convert to Hindutva, is now a member of the BJP think-tank and he has put his passionate belief in Hindutva in print in *The Saffron Book*.

Like other supporters of Hindutva, Goradia attributes anti-Muslim feelings in the minds of this generation of Hindus to the vandalism of Muslim invaders from Mahmud Ghazni onwards and the destruction of temples during the reign of Aurangzeb. He asserts that this makes Hindu blood boil with anger. How long can we allow our blood to boil and what will be its consequences on the health of the nation? Goradia concedes that perpetuating hatred against present-day Muslims for what their forefathers did centuries ago will be counter-productive. His solution is, however, naive and beyond belief. He writes: 'One simple way would be to call a congress of leading Muslim lights of India, say one hundred of them, maybe more. Let them consider seven of the desecrations described in this volume and let them give back these sites on their own as these leave no doubt of the wrongs committed.'

Goradia must know there is no possibility whatsoever of such a conclave of Muslim leaders being convened or their magnanimously handing over mosques in which prayers have been offered over hundreds of years. Indeed, never was this kind of demand articulated till the Sangh parivar gained ascendancy in Indian politics. Goradia doesn't only ask for the noses of Indian Muslims to be rubbed in the dirt of the past. He has similar reservations about Christian presence in India, about the demise of Nehruvian secularism and socialism and about much else. His book deserves to be read because it gives us an insight into the minds of Hindu fundamentalists.

When the likes of Praveen Togadia and Giriraj Kishore criticize the three-man Election Commission (of whom two are Hindus), they single out J.M. Lyngdoh because he is a Christian and describe him as 'anti-Hindu'. I want to yell back at these fellows: 'Lyngdoh is not anti-Hindu. He is a civilized gentleman, above communal prejudices. It is people like you who are anti-Hindu because you give Hinduism a bad name.'

If fundamentalists have any religion at all, it is hate. Abuse and lies come more easily to them than reason and logic. Their private armies are designed to implement political agendas through force and to be used in communal riots. It is the job of the courts and the police, and not of illiterate sadhus and armed thugs, to uphold and enforce law and order. But that is clearly not the BJP's idea of good governance.

Until a few years ago I used to think that I could dismiss the menace of fascism erupting in my own country as a figment of my sick mind. I can no longer do so. The Indian brand of fascism is at our doorstep. The chief apologist for Indian fascism is Deputy Prime Minister L.K. Advani, who read Adolf Hitler's *Mein Kampf* while in jail during the Emergency. Bharatiya fascism has its crudest protagonists in Bal Thackeray, the Shiv Sena supremo who openly praises Hitler as a superman. Its chief executioner is Narendra Modi, chief minister of Gujarat. And of course, there is the rag-tag of the Singhals, Giriraj Kishores, Togadias and other tuppenny-ha'penny rabble-rousers.

Germany was a literate nation and yet succumbed to the most irrational sort of racial prejudice. We are largely illiterate and it is much easier to sway our masses by rousing their basest instincts. Distort facts, inject dollops of pride in your own race and religion, and prejudice and contempt for that of others, and you have a witches' brew of hate which can be easily brought to a boil. We saw how Bhindranwale succeeded in winning over the Sikh masses by preaching hate. We are now witness to the same kind of preaching of hate on a national scale. The Nazis had Jews and Gypsies as their targets. Our fascists have all religious minorities as theirs. No better proof of this is needed than BJP chief Venkaiah Naidu's spirited defence of Modi's hate speeches against the Muslims and the atrocities against them by his supporters. Naidu said that the Congress has no right to accuse Modi of the mass killing of Muslims when its own hands are soiled by the blood of innocent Sikhs massacred in 1984. Clearly, minorities are fair game for both sides.

The BJP and its sister organizations incite the majority Hindus by harping on the anti-Hindu acts of the medieval Islamic rulers of India. But our entire history is that of a people divided by race and religion with each section trying to dominate the other by violence and vandalism. No group can point an accusing finger at the other. If the Muslims killed and destroyed, the non-Muslims (the Raiputs, Jats, Marathas and Sikhs) did no less. Our history is not the simple annals of Hindu-Muslim confrontation. In most if not all cases of conflicts, there were Hindus on the side of Muslims and Muslims on the side of Hindus. Through all the centuries of Hindu-Muslim association runs a strand of mutual respect and affection which made it possible for us to create a common culture. The Qutab Minar, the Taj Mahal and Fatehpur Sikri, though essentially Saracenic in concept (you can see the similarity in hundreds of mosques and mausoleums in West Asia), were often executed by Hindu artists and craftsmen and therefore became a Hindu-Muslim mélange which we can rightly describe as Indian. It is both historically wrong and morally unfair to cater to chauvinistic pride and prejudice. If we brainwash the younger generation with this venomous mixture of distorted fact, fancy and specious argument, we will forever be the real authors of communal discord. If we fail to hold ourselves as one nation, we will be the authors of that failure. And we will be the real perpetrators of the end of India.

Hate-mongers & Co. Pvt. Ltd

What exactly is the nature of the beast at our door? An examination of the RSS and its ideology is important to get a true sense of the danger we are in. But before I do that, I would like to describe a meeting I had thirty years ago with Madhavrao Sadasivrao Golwalkar, the then head of the RSS. Thinking back on it, I realize that part of the Sangh parivar's success can be attributed to the charm and charisma of many of its leaders. They were men of polite manner, obvious sophistication and intelligence who cloaked their fascist ideas in sweet reasonableness and impeccable etiquette.

Guru Golwalkar had long been on the top of my hate list, because I could not forget the RSS's role in communal riots, the assassination of the Mahatma and its attempt to change India from a secular State to a Hindu rashtra. There were passages in his 1939 tract, *We, or Our Nationhood Defined*, that seemed to suggest that he shared Hitler's ideas about racial purity and approved of his methods to purge Germany of the Jews. I could not resist the chance of meeting him and in November 1972, I interviewed him for *The Illustrated Weekly*:

'I expect to run into a cordon of uniformed swayam sevaks. There are none; not even plainclothes CIDs to take down the number of my car. I arrive at what looks like a middle-class apartment. It seems as though there is a puja going on inside—there are rows of sandals outside, the fragrance of agarbatti, the bustle of women behind the scenes, the tinkle of utensils and crockery. I step inside.

'It is a small room in which sit a dozen men in spotless white kurtas and dhotis—all looking newly washed as only Maharashtrian Brahmins can manage to make them look. And there is Guru Golwalkar: a frail man in his mid-sixties, black hair curling to his shoulders, a moustache covering his mouth, a wispy grey beard dangling down his chin. He wears an inerasable smile and dark eyes twinkle through his bifocals. He looks like an Indian Ho Chi Minh. For a man who has only recently undergone surgery for breast cancer, he is remarkably fit and cheerful. Being a guru, I feel he may expect a chela-like obeisance. He does not give me a chance. As I bend to touch his feet, he grasps my hands in his bony fingers and pulls me down on the seat beside him.

"'I am very glad to meet you," he says. "I had been wanting to do so for some time." His Hindi is very shudh.

'"Me too," I reply clumsily. "Ever since I read your *Bunch of Letters*."

'"*Bunch of Thoughts*," he corrects me. He does not want to know my views on it.

'He takes one of my hands in his and pats it. "So?" he looks inquiringly at me.

'"I don't know where to begin. I am told you shun publicity and your organization is secret."

'"It is true we do not seek publicity but there is nothing secret about us. Ask me anything you want to."

'"I read about your movement in Jack Curran's *The RSS and Hindu Militarism*. He says . . ."

'"It is a biased account," interrupts Guruji. "Unfair, inaccurate—he misquoted me and many others. There is no militarism in our movement. We value discipline—which is a different matter."

'I tell him that I had read an article describing Curran as the head of CIA operations in Europe and Africa. "I would never have suspected it," I say very naively. "I have known him for twenty years."

'Guruji beams a smile at me. "This doesn't surprise me at all." I do not know whether his remark is a comment on Curran being a part of the CIA or my naiveté.

"'There is one thing which bothers me about the RSS. If you permit me, I will put it as bluntly as I can."

"'Go ahead."

"'It is your attitude towards the minorities, particularly the Christians and the Muslims."

"'We have nothing against the Christians expect their methods of gaining converts. When they give medicines to the sick or bread to the hungry, they should not exploit the situation by propagating their religion to those people. I am glad there is a move to make the Indian churches autonomous and independent of Rome."

'"What about the Muslims?"

'"What about them?"

'I have no doubt in my mind that the dual loyalties that many Muslims have towards both India and Pakistan is due to historical factors for which Hindus are as much to blame as they. It also stems from a feeling of insecurity that they have been made to suffer since Partition. In any case, one cannot hold the entire community responsible for the wrongs of a few.

'"Guruji, there are six crore Indian Muslims here with us." I get eloquent. "We cannot eliminate them, we cannot drive them out, we cannot convert them. This is their home. We must reassure them—make them feel wanted. Let us win them over with love. This should be an article of . . ."

"'I would reverse the order," he interrupts. "As a matter of fact I would say the only right policy towards Muslims is to win their loyalty by love."

'I am startled. Is he playing with words? Or does he really mean what he says? He qualifies his statement: "A delegation of the Jamat-i-Islami came to see me. I told them that Muslims must forget that they ruled India. They should not look upon foreign Muslim countries as their homelands. They must join the mainstream of Indianism."

"'How?"

'"We should explain things to them. Sometimes one feels angry with Muslims for what they do, but then Hindu blood never harbours ill-will for very long. Time is a great healer. I am an optimist and feel that Hinduism and Islam will learn to live with each other."

'Tea is served. Guruji's glass mug provides a diversion. I ask him why he doesn't drink the beverage out of porcelain like the rest of us. He smiles. "I have always taken it in this mug. I take it with me wherever I go." His closest companion, Dr Thatte, who has dedicated his life to the RSS, explains: "Porcelain wears off and exposes the clay beneath. Clay can harbour germs."

'I return to my theme.

'"Why do you pin your faith on religion when most of the world is turning irreligious and agnostic?"

'"Hinduism is on firm ground because it has no dogma. It has had agnostics before; it will survive the wave of irreligiousness better than any other religious system."

'"How can you say that? The evidence is the other way. The only religions which are standing firm and even increasing their hold on the people are those based on dogma—Catholicism, and more than Catholicism, Islam."

'"It is a passing phase. Agnosticism will overtake them; it will not overtake

Hinduism. Ours is not a religion in the dictionary sense of the word; it is dharma, a way of life. Hinduism will take agnosticism in its stride."

'I have taken more than half an hour of Guruji's time. He shows no sign of impatience. When I ask for leave, he again grasps my hands to prevent me from touching his feet.'

I remember being impressed with Guru Golwalkar because he did not try to persuade me to agree with his point of view. He had made me feel that he was open to persuasion. I accepted his invitation to visit him in Nagpur and see things for myself. I had thought then that I could perhaps bring him around to making Hindu-Muslim unity the main aim of his RSS. I had been a simple-minded Sardar.

The Sangh parivar's PR men can no longer hide the truth about their mission. And the truth is this: the Rashtriya Swayamsevak Sangh stands for 'the spread of Hindu culture'. This 'culture' is 'a value system' based on Savarkar's concept of Hindutva and is necessarily a Hindu value system. The mission of the RSS is to 'unite and rejuvenate our nation on the sound foundation of Dharma', a mission that can be achieved by 'a strong and united Hindu society'. It has therefore undertaken the task of uniting the Hindus because it believes that 'rejuvenation of the Hindu nation is in the interest of the whole humanity (sic)'. Clearly, there is no room here for anyone who does not pray to Hindu gods.

The RSS is blatantly and fiercely anti-Muslim and anti-Christian. It junks Jesus just as it rejects roza. Golwalkar even raised an objection when Abdul Hamid and the Keelor bothers were honoured by the Indian government for their bravery during the Indo-Pak war—the gallant men were non-Hindus.

Apart from the assassination of the Mahatma, the RSS, VHP, BJP and RSS offshoots like the Bajrang Dal and Vanavasi Kalyan Ashram have been implicated in various communal riots all over the country. The RSS ally Shiv Sena, with its leader Bal Thackeray, believes in 'benign dictatorship' for India. BJP leaders like the late Vijaya Raje Scindia were in favour of inhuman practices like sati and believed in the Hindu caste system. Every year, 14 February, St. Valentine's Day, is marked by Shiv Sena sainiks going on a rampage all over the country. They burn buses, vandalize shops and generally make a nuisance of themselves protesting against what they call 'cultural decadence'. They wish to protect a Hindu rashtra from the evil influence of Western practices.

We talk about the Taliban using religion to stifle the social and cultural lives of the people of Afghanistan. The same thing has been happening in our very homeland and we see it in every aspect of our daily life. It is not only the Shiv Sena that foams at the mouth about 'Western influence', Minister of State for Tourism and Cultural Affairs Bhavnaben Chikalia was recently considering banning discotheques in all government hotels. She felt it was 'against our culture' and a 'bad influence on our Bharatiya sanskriti'. Some years ago, Sushma Swaraj made a hue and cry about Fashion Television, and the Sangh agitated all over the country against Deepa Mehta's *Fire* and even succeeded in stopping *Water*, her next film, about the widows of Varanasi. These moral police have problems with books, with plays, with music and with art. In their effort to create a Hindu rashtra, they have played up the Shah Bano case, using the Congress's appeasement of the Muslim orthodoxy as their trump card. They have attempted to 'rectify' Muslim 'wrongs' in history by rewriting it. They have tampered with textbooks in their efforts to 'amend' Leftist readings and tried to reconstruct in the twenty-first century an imagined Hindu golden age.

Every fascist regime needs communities and groups it can demonize in order to thrive. It starts with one group or two. But it never ends there. A movement built on hate can only sustain itself by continually creating fear and strife. Those of us today who feel secure because we are not Muslims or Christians are living in a fool's paradise. The Sangh is already targeting Leftist historians and 'Westernized' youth. Tomorrow it will turn its hate on women who wear skirts, people who eat meat, drink liquor, watch foreign films, don't go on annual pilgrimages to temples, use toothpaste instead of danth manjan, prefer allopathic doctors to vaids, kiss or shake hands in greeting instead of shouting 'Jai Shri Ram . . .' No one is safe. We must realize this if we hope to keep India alive.

COMMUNALISM—AN OLD PROBLEM

'It has more arms than an octopus,' thundered Qazi Abdul Sattar, professor of Urdu at Aligarh Muslim University. We were at a seminar in Kanpur in late 2002. Amongst the others on the rostrum were the writers Rajendra Yadav and Krishna Sobti and the saffron-clad sadhu-politician Swami Agnivesh. There was a gory opening to the seminar. Police bandobast around the Merchant Chambers Hall almost got into disarray when a senior head constable ticked off an errant junior for neglecting his duty. The junior rewarded his superior by putting a bullet through his heart. We proceeded to discuss the menace of communalism as if nothing had happened.

The audience was most receptive; comparing communalism to the tentacles of an octopus drew cries of wah! wah! 'Who was the admiral of Shivaji's fleet?' asked Qazi Sahib. And answered the question himself: 'A Muslim.' He carried Shivaji's flags of secularism further. 'Who was the commander of Shivaji's artillery? A Muslim. When Shivaji sacked Surat he brought back a copy of the Holy Quran bearing it reverently on his head.' So great was Qazi Sahib's enthusiasm for the Maratha hero that he made him out as the vanquisher of the communal villain, Aurangzeb. I had not read of it in any book of history but in that atmosphere, sentiment mattered more than historic facts.

We all talked a lot and were applauded. We slew the canker of communalism ending on the note that all the world is communal save thee and me, and even thee is a little communal. We went back to our business the next day and nothing changed with the world.

Qazi Sattar was right in saying that communalism is a many-armed octopus. And just as an octopus, when attacked, squirts ink to obscure the vision of its assailant, the communalist spreads canards which put attackers off his trail and make his victims let down their guard. These canards are sometimes borrowed from die-hard Gandhians who often ignore hard reality. One such belief which the communalists use to their advantage is in Hindu-Muslim bhai-bhaism: we are all children of the one God who is both Ishwar and Allah, Ram and Rahim, ergo, Hindus and Muslims and Christians are brothers. The truth is that wherever people of different races, religions, languages and cultures have co-existed, instead of bhai-bhaism there is tension. And if land, property or business is involved, tension often explodes into violence. The other canard is that there were no communal riots before the British introduced their policy of divide and rule. In fact, Hindu-Muslim tensions have existed since Islam came to India. And before Islam there were conflicts between Hindus and Jains, Hindus and Buddhists, Dravidians and Aryans.

It is wrong and counter-productive to pretend that communalism is something the Sangh parivar invented in India. The Sangh's genius was in creating a monster out of existing prejudices. The Congress, especially under Indira Gandhi, played its own dirty role. The

BJP is only more dangerous because of its brazenness. It is more dangerous because it uses democracy to camouflage its fascist agenda. But everybody has blood on his hands. Every religious or ethnic group in India can and has been incited to kill and plunder. The most gruesome example of this was what happened at Nellie in Assam in 1983. There, over 3,000 men, women and children were slain in one long orgy of killing. Bangladeshi refugees killed Bengalis and Assamese, Assamese and Bengalis killed each other, tribals killed non-tribals, Muslims killed Hindus and Christians, and Christians killed Hindus. In short, it was just about everyone killing everyone else.

It would be naive to believe that communalism can be banished simply by voting the BJP out of power. The problem is much larger, and though it has assumed diabolical proportions today because of the BJP's politics, it has been around for a very long time. We must not miss the wood for the trees.

A Brief History of Communalism

Over two thousand years ago, Buddhism was on the ascendant in India. Emperor Ashoka was the most famous convert to Buddhism. When Brahminical Hinduism gained favour again with ruling dynasties, especially in the ninth and tenth centuries, Buddhists were persecuted and their places of worship demolished. Later, in the reign of many Muslim rulers, Hindus were discriminated against and their temples destroyed.

The British followed a policy of divide and rule, but in India it was never difficult to divide. There were Hindu-Muslim riots every now and then and that suited the British fine as long as there was no threat to their empire. The Christians, naturally, felt more secure during British rule. But there was no religious persecution. The discrimination was based on race.

With Independence came Partition and the worst communal violence in India's history. I was a witness to that madness, and I thought the nation was coming to an end. In the first week of August 1947, I was in Lahore. In the second half of the same month I was in Delhi. I did not know which country I belonged to— India or Pakistan. I was born in a village deep in the heart of what became Pakistan. I expected to live the rest of my life in Lahore. I sympathized with Muslims who wanted a separate state of their own, and had reconciled myself to living and prospering in that Muslim state. I was not given the choice. A week before I left Lahore, my neighbours on either side had declared their religious identities in large letters and symbols painted on their walls. The wall of the house on my left bore the legend in Urdu: Parsee ka makaan. The other wall had huge crosses painted on it to indicate that the residents were Christians. They need not have taken the trouble. Gangs from nearby Mozang had started marking out Hindu and Sikh homes for loot and forcible occupation. It was made abundantly clear to me that I was not wanted in Pakistan, for no other reason than that I was a Sikh.

On the other side of the new border, Hindus and Sikhs outdid their fellow goons of West Punjab. In the east, the prolonged Hindu-Muslim riots in Calcutta led to massacres of

Muslims in Bihar, followed by massacres of Hindus in Noakhali in East Bengal. Waves of Hindus and Sikhs fled across the borders to safety. Many were butchered on the way.

For some time the shock of having been deprived of my home and belongings and the tragedy of civil strife that took thousands of lives and left millions homeless was forgotten in the euphoria of the newly won Independence. I was one of the vast crowd milling around Parliament House on the midnight of 14/15 August 1947. In rapt silence we heard Sucheta Kripalani sing *Vande Mataram* and Pandit Nehru's 'Tryst with destiny' speech. We were there till the early hours of the morning, shouting ourselves hoarse with slogans like *Bharat mata ki jai* and *Mahatma Gandhi ki jai*. It was great to be alive.

When the moment passed, the truth slowly dawned on me. Was this the kind of Independence we were looking forward to? Faiz Ahmed Faiz's lines written in August 1947 came to mind:

> *Yeh daagh daagh ujaala, yeh shab*
> *guzeeda seher*
> *Voh jis ka intizaar tha ham ko, yeh*
> *voh seher to   nahin;*
> *Yeh voh seher to nahin jis kee aarzoo*
> *lay kar*
> *Chaley thhey yaar ke mil jaaegee*
> *kaheen na kaheen*
> *Falak kay dasht mein taaron kee*
> *aakhree manzil.*

> (This dawn dappled with shades of
>   twilight;
> This is not the dawn for which we
>   waited all night;

This is not the dawn that we had
  hoped for

When we comrades set out on our
  march in the hope

That somewhere in the vast wilderness
  of the sky

We will find our final destination
  beyond the stars.)

I was luckier than most of the millions of refugees who had trekked out of Pakistan, having lost everything they owned, and many of whose relations had been murdered or their womenfolk kidnapped and raped. I had my parents' home to come to. And soon I got a job with the Ministry of External Affairs. But memories of the Partition massacres continued to haunt me. I was reminded of Amrita Pritam's immortal lament which invokes the spirit of

Punjab's most famous balladeer, Waris Shah, the author of the epic poem *Heer Ranjah*:

> *Aj aakhaan Warris Shah noo*
>
> *Utth kabaraan vicchon bol;*
>
> *Ik roee see dhee Punjab dee*
>
> *Toun likh likh maarey vain,*
>
> *Aj lakhaan dheeaan rondian*
>
> *Tainee Warris Shah noon kehan*
>
> *O, dardmandaan day dardeeya utth*
>   *tak apna Punjab*
>
> *Beyley laashaan vicchiyaan, lahoo da*
>   *bharya Chenab.*

(I ask Warris Shah, rise from your
    grave and speak!

When one daughter of the Punjab wept

You wrote a string of lamentations;

Today a hundred thousands are in
    tears

Plead with you as they cry

O, comforter of the suffering, come
    and see your Punjab

Corpses are strewn about the fields,
    blood flows in the Chenab.)

Independent India began limping back to health. I thought we had seen the worst and hoped that the one thing that would never happen again was Hindu-Muslim riots. The British had kept the communities apart to perpetuate their rule. Now that they were gone, we would evolve a common Indian identity overriding religious, linguistic and caste divisions. I hoped that the massive bloodletting of Partition would have taken all the venom of communal hatred out of our bodies.

Alas! After a lull of a few years, the communal virus erupted again in different parts of the country. Commissions of inquiry have stated in categorical terms that in all Hindu-Muslim riots after Independence, over seventy-five per cent of casualties—in terms of life and property—were Muslim. I have little faith in the impartiality of our police in quelling communal violence but I had hoped for better performance from the majority community. It has failed in its duty and politicians have taken advantage of this.

From the time Indira Gandhi became Prime Minister religion began to encroach on the political domain. Religion- and community-based political parties began to exploit religious and communal sentiments to gain political leverage. They succeeded beyond their own wildest dreams. We have come to such a pass that it would not be an exaggeration to describe Indian secularism as only notional—*naam kay vaastey*. During British rule communal violence was limited to Hindu-Muslim confrontations on religious holidays like Holi, Id-ul Zuha, the Ganapati festival. Riots occurred in a few riot-prone towns. Today, riots take place between Hindus and Muslims, Hindus and Sikhs, Hindus and Christians, caste-Hindus and Harijans, tribals and non-tribals, Bengalis and Assamese, Maharashtrians and Kannadigas. The entire country has become riot-prone. Everyone's hand rises against his neighbour because everyone wants what his neighbour has—his land, his job, or his business. Racial, religious and linguistic differences provide the excuse to do so. The instigation usually comes from the educated middle class of tradesmen (incidentally, the constituency of the BJP) and politicians (except perhaps the communists); their instruments are lumpen elements and the educated-unemployed and, as Gujarat showed us in 2002, the dispossessed who can be swayed by a dangerous cocktail of passionate rhetoric, attractive lies, and plain hard cash.

The Punjab Example

For anyone interested in understanding the persistence of communal feelings among Indians and the tragic results of letting them grow unchecked or encouraging them, Punjab makes for a good case study. I use Punjab as an example because it is home to the community I know best. Also because through history, Punjab has suffered more than any other Indian state due to religious conflict.

The Punjabis of today are what they are because of the legacy their forefathers left them. They had to face invasions by tribesmen of Central Asia and beyond. Recorded in history are the invasions by Greeks under Alexander. From AD 1000 onwards, came invaders like Ghazni, Ghauri, and the conquering dynasties—the Tughlaqs, the Lodhis and then the Mughals. When the Mughal empire began to totter, came Nadir Shah and his Afghan successor, Ahmed Shah Abdali, who invaded India nine times in quick succession, laying bare the countryside and Delhi. Punjabis bore the brunt of these invasions and the humiliations which followed in their wake. It took centuries of periodic depredations for the people of Punjab to realize that they must stand together in order to be able to resist and, if possible, repel invaders.

Although by this time more than half of the people of the region had converted to Islam, they were willing to join hands with Hindus and Sikhs. An important factor in this was the new Sikh religion, born of the need to bring the Hindu and Muslim communities together. The new faith borrowed elements from both Hinduism and Islam—an edifice built as it were with Hindu bricks and Muslim mortar. The founder of Sikhism, Guru Nanak (1469-1539), came to be acclaimed by both communities. A popular couplet describes him as:

> *Guru Nanak Shah Fakir*
>
> *Hindu ka Guru, Mussalman ka Pir.*
>
> (Guru Nanak, the King of Fakirs,
>
> To the Hindu a Guru, to the Muslim
>   a Pir.)

The spirit of Punjabi nationality, *Punjabiyat*, was thus born. It did not, of course, resolve all conflict. Sikhs, in fact, soon found themselves the target of Mughal anger. The Mughal empire was naturally concerned by the growing popularity of the Sikh Gurus, whom they saw as leaders of a cult with political ambitions. Punjab was too important a region for them. The Sikh gurus and their followers were persecuted. The reason was clearly more political than religious. The fifth Guru, Arjun, was executed by the Muslim rulers in Lahore. With this began the transformation of the Sikhs into a militant sect. Under the last Guru, Gobind Singh, whose father, Guru Tegh Bahadur, was executed in Delhi, this transformation was complete.

There was tension between the Hindu Brahmin order and the Sikhs too. Many of Guru Nanak's teachings went against entrenched Hindu beliefs and attitudes, like idol-worship, religious ritual and the caste system. Hindu rulers of the hill kingdoms in and around Punjab perceived the Sikhs, sometimes rightly, as a threat and often colluded with Mughal forces in their campaigns against them. Sikh historians maintain that among the tormentors of Guru Arjun, who was executed by the Mughals, was a Hindu banker whose daughter's hand Arjun had refused to accept for his son. There are also historical records that say that Guru Gobind Singh's sons, who were captured and killed by Mughal forces, were betrayed by their Brahmin servant.

Despite this, there was no serious rift between the Muslims and Hindus and Sikhs in Punjab. The spirit of Punjabi nationalism survived. It took the genius of Maharaja Ranjit Singh to harness this emotion and create a truly Punjabi kingdom. Among his principal advisers were Muslims, Hindus and Sikhs. Likewise, his army, trained by Europeans, comprised all three: his artillery was commanded by General Elahi Baksh, his cavalry consisted mainly of Sikh horsemen, his infantry was a mix of Hindus, Sikhs, Muslims and Gurkhas. General Diwan Chand captured the fort of Multan for him. Hari Singh Nalwa and Akali Phula Singh reduced the turbulent tribesmen of the north-west frontier to submission. Punjabi Muslims fought shoulder to shoulder with their Punjabi brethren against Muslim Pathans and Afghans. It was a remarkable achievement. Ranjit Singh was the first Indian in a thousand years to stem the tides of invasions across the north-west frontier.

The year Ranjit Singh died, his Muslim troops, led by Colonel Shaikh Basawan, carried Ranjit Singh's colours through the streets of Kabul in a victory parade. A couple of years later,

Zoravar Singh, a Dogra Hindu, planted Ranjit Singh's flag in the heart of Tibet. It is significant that the only person to make an attempt on Ranjit Singh's life was a Sikh.

The British annexed the Sikh kingdom in 1849. They successfully split the three communities apart by giving preferential treatment to Punjabi Muslims and Sikhs (only the Khalsas) at the expense of the Punjabi Hindus. Special electorates and reservation of seats in elected bodies were given to Muslims and Sikhs in excess of their numbers. Punjabi Mussalmans and Khalsa Sikhs were declared 'martial races' for recruitment to the army or the police; only one small Hindu caste, the Mohyal Brahmins, qualified as martial. Seeds of division sowed by the British sprouted and split the three communities.

As the freedom movement picked up all over India, Punjabis lagged behind. Initially, the Punjab Congress consisted largely of urban Hindus. After the Akali agitation of the 1920s, Sikhs began to join it in larger numbers. With a few notable exceptions like Dr Alam and Saifuddin Kitchlu, Punjabi Muslims kept aloof. This was roughly the situation on the eve of Independence. Punjabi Muslims wanted the partition of the country and an independent state, Pakistan. Punjabi Hindus and Sikhs opposed it and were expelled. Punjab paid a very heavy price for Partition. Almost ten million people lost their lands, homes and belongings, while almost a million lost their lives in the communal strife that came with it.

India was able to accommodate five million Hindu and Sikh Punjabi refugees. Sikh farmers took over the small holdings of the Muslims who had fled East Punjab. These Sikh refugees had left behind large agricultural land irrigated by canals. What they got was no more than thirty acres irrigated by well water. They made the arid wastes of Ganganagar district of Rajasthan and swamplands of the Terai, the most prosperous regions of India. In East Punjab, which came in the Indian share, a few years after the setting up of the Punjab Agricultural University in 1962, the average yield of wheat and rice was three times the yield of all of Pakistan. The Green Revolution was largely the achievement of Sikh farmers. More remarkable was the fact that while Hindu and Sikh refugees who migrated from Pakistan were readily and painlessly integrated as Indians, Muslim refugees who migrated from India to Pakistan are still referred to as *Mohajirs* and locals do not intermingle with them. Yet more remarkable was the fact that though migrating Punjabis were reduced to penury, it was rare to see a Punjabi beg for alms.

Despite the prosperity, post-Partition Punjab has a wounded history. There came the serious rift between Hindus and Sikhs, two communities who had *roti-beti ke rishte*, who broke bread together and gave their daughters in marriage to each other's families. When Sikhs demanded a Punjabi-speaking state, many Punjabi Hindus were persuaded by Hindu communal groups to declare to census officials that their mother tongue was Hindi. Sikhs who clamoured for the new state in reality wanted a Sikh-majority state and used the linguistic argument as a sugar-coating. But logic was on their side and after prolonged agitation, their demand was conceded. Himachal and Haryana were separated from old Punjab and a purely

Punjabi-speaking state came into being. Sixty per cent of the Punjabi-speaking population of present-day Punjab is Sikh, forty per cent Hindu.

Hindu-Sikh tensions continued to bedevil the Punjab. They came to a head with the rise of Sikh fundamentalism under Jarnail Singh Bhindranwale, who led terrorist activities aimed against Punjabi Hindus in the early 1980s. The Bhindranwale chapter in Indian history is a perfect illustration of the disastrous results of not keeping politics separate from religion. Bhindranwale was a creation of the Congress and the Akalis. Indira Gandhi was advised by Zail Singh that this small-time kattar (hardline) Sikh preacher should be built up as a leader to counter the ruling Akalis in Punjab. Later, the Akalis tried to woo Bhindranwale away from their rivals and propped him up. Sant Longowal once described him as *saadda danda* (our stick) to beat the Congress government with. In time he became a monster who would turn around and destroy the very people who created him and plunge Punjab and much of the country into chaos.

Bhindranwale's popularity among the Sikhs has an interesting lesson for our times, when Hindu fundamentalists are becoming increasingly popular among middle-class Hindus who are materially better off now than they have ever been. Believe it or not, one main reason for the rise of Bhindranwale was the prosperity that came to Punjab with the Green Revolution. With prosperity came sudden changes, Western influences, a crisis of identity, and degeneration—alcoholism, smoking, drug addiction, gambling, blue films, fornication. The worst sufferers were women and children, wives and offspring of peasants who could not digest their sudden prosperity. On this scene came Bhindranwale preaching against these evils and carried on a vigorous campaign of 'Amritprachar'.

Everywhere he went, he baptised Sikhs by the thousands and made them swear in front of congregations that they would never again touch intoxicants and pornography or adopt Western ways. They did not break their oath. Money previously squandered was saved. Time previously wasted in drink and drugs was now spent on more careful tillage—bringing more money. Bhindranwale saved a large section of Sikh peasantry from rack and ruin.

It was their women and children who acclaimed him as a saviour and a saint: he was a good guy. To this image, Bhindranwale put on the macho gloss of a tough man: bandolier charged with bullets across his hairy chest, pistol on his hip, in his hand a silver arrow like the one Maharaja Ranjit Singh used to carry. The crowds loved him when he referred to Indira Gandhi as *pandit dee dhee* (that daughter of a Brahmin—much milder than what Praveen Togadia has called Sonia Gandhi in recent times) and the central government as *bania-Hindu sarkar*. Unemployed young men who passed out of college but could not be absorbed into their ancestral farming business were impressed by his fiery speeches and became his followers.

Later when Bhindranwale shifted to the Golden Temple, started making anti-Hindu speeches and his goons began killing innocent people, his admirers dismissed the allegations as government propaganda. To them he still remained a good guy. Even as Hindus were being pulled out of buses and being shot and transistor bombs were going off in crowded markets all over north India, Sikh pride was at its height.

The year 1984 witnessed the bloodiest confrontation between Bhindranwale's followers and the Central government when the Indian Army entered the Golden Temple at Amritsar and destroyed the Akal Takht. Almost 5,000 men and women, mostly innocent pilgrims who were there on the martyrdom day of Guru Arjun Dev, the founder of the Temple, were killed in the crossfire between Bhindranwale's men and the Army. A few months later, on 31 October, Indira Gandhi was slain by one of her Sikh bodyguards. Terrible results followed. In towns and cities across the Gangetic plain down to Karnataka, frenzied mobs, often led by Congress leaders, took a heavy toll of Sikh life and property.

In Delhi alone, over 3,000 Sikhs were burnt alive and over seventy gurudwaras wrecked. On the afternoon of 31 October, I saw a huge cloud of black smoke billowing out from Connaught Circus. Sikh property in the area had been set on fire. In the evening I saw hooligans wreck Sikh-owned taxis parked outside Ambassador Hotel and ransack Sikh shops in Khan Market, a stone's throw from my house. I saw two lines of policemen under an officer across the road. They were armed, but stood idly watching the looters on rampage.

At midnight I was woken up by slogan-shouting: 'Khoon ka badla khoon say lengey.' Blood for blood. I ran out into my back garden and through the boundary hedge I saw a

truckload of men armed with lathis and cans
of oil attack the Sujan Singh Park gurudwara
and set fire to a few cars left for servicing in
the garage run by Sikh mechanics.

Although I had anticipated some spontaneous
outburst of anger against Sikhs because of
what Bhindranwale's men had been doing to
innocent Hindus in Punjab, what happened in
Delhi was organized. The entire government
machinery went into voluntary paralysis. No
curfew was imposed, no order to shoot at sight
was carried out.

It was not a communal riot because in many
areas Hindus came to the rescue of their Sikh
neighbours. Also, there was no retaliation
against Hindus by Sikhs in Punjab. The finger
of suspicion clearly pointed at one party for
giving the signal 'Teach the Sikhs a lesson.'

Nineteen eighty-four was the worst ever year for the Sikhs since they lost their kingdom 133 years ago. For years after the pogrom, no one was convicted. There were many commissions that went over the events of the two days. Non-official commissions led by eminent men like Justice Tarkunde, Dr Kothari and retired Chief Justice of the Supreme Court S.M. Sikri roundly condemned the govenment of the day. They even named several MPs of the Congress for having instigated violence against a hapless and vastly outnumbered minority which had never had the slightest sense of insecurity in its relationship with the Hindus. But the official commission exonerated the Congress and the government of all blame. To this day Congress leaders who led the mobs live as free men.

The country paid a heavy price for 1984. But the events of Gujarat prove that neither the political parties nor the people of India have learnt any lessons from that. We are condemned to repeat history.

Not Just the BJP

It would be in all our interests to remember that what the BJP has perfected began under the Congress. Before Gujarat, the worst example of police connivance with terrorism was witnessed during the two days following the assassination of Mrs Gandhi. N.S. Saksena, a retired Director General of Police, wrote in his book *Terrorism: History and Facts in the World and in India*: 'The police in Delhi, Kanpur, Gaziabad, etc., was under the impression that anti-Sikh riots had the approval of the government.' The then home minister admitted in Parliament that over 2,400 persons were killed in Delhi alone. (The real figure was much higher.) The Delhi police registered only 359 cases. The magistracy proved equally compliant: Ninety-nine per cent of the accused charged with these unbailable offences were released on bail and they terrorized relatives of the very people they killed and molested from giving evidence against them. Saksena astutely observed that 'terrorism has largely been a public sector enterprise'.

What could have been put down by a firm hand in a few hours was deliberately allowed to go on for seventy-two hours. Far from condemning it, in his first public oration as prime minister, Rajiv Gandhi explained it away: 'When a big tree falls, the earth about it shakes.' The conduct of the Congress in the elections that followed was equally reprehensible. Its posters had a distinctly anti-

Sikh bias. For example, the ad 'Do you feel safe in a taxi driven by a member of another community?' In his own constituency, Amethi, where Rajiv had his Sikh sister-in-law Maneka opposing him, one of the slogans chanted was: *Beti hai Sardar ki, qaum hai ghaddar ki* (She is the daughter of a Sikh, she belongs to a community of traitors). The Congress party won its landslide victory on a wave of anti-Sikh sentiment generated by it.

But 1984 was not the only case of communal violence during Congress rule. The record of Congress governments in the states ruled by it has been generally abysmal. The cold-blooded shooting down of over seventy Muslim peasants in Hashimpura, anti-Muslim riots in Ahmedabad, in Bhiwandi and Jalgaon, in the towns of Madhya Pradesh, and in Bhagalpur, give the lie to the Congress's secular credentials.

One should not judge political parties by the labels they wear on their lapels or by the high-sounding manifestos issued by them, but by their actions. I will concede that Muslims have never had it as bad as now, when the BJP is in power. But they were never allowed to flourish under Congress rule either. Indira Gandhi and then Rajiv used the Muslim community as a vote bank. They weren't interested in their future as Indian citizens. They ensured that like the Dalits, Indian Muslims remained poor and insecure, so they could be fooled into seeing the Congress as their only saviour.

I remember a visit to Aligarh in the mid 1970s. What I saw there sums up what the Congress had done for the Muslims of India. Driving back to Delhi after a brief stay at the Aligarh Muslim University, I had a glimpse of the 'progress' made by the Muslim peasantry. Some miles from Ghaziabad were a few villages entirely inhabited by Muslims. I went through the largest one called Dasna. Its population: 2,300. The homes looked clean enough but the lanes were incredibly filthy. Drains clogged with evil-smelling slime. A few electric lights. But though everyone was within calling distance, there was a loudspeaker attached to the minaret of the mosque. I saw the only school at Dasna, a high school; but I was told that no more than thirty children went to it. 'What will they do with education?' asked a young man whose family was one of the three in the entire area that owned a tractor. 'They learn the Quran Sharif at the mosque and that is enough. And we do not believe in education for girls.' The Tehsildars accompanying me told me that in the last family planning drive in the region, not one male or female in the collection of villages around Dasna had volunteered for vasectomy or hysterectomy.

By encouraging regressive mullahs and orthodox leaders and treating Indian Muslims as a homogeneous mass, the Congress consigned the whole community to an intellectual and social ghetto. The Muslim closed his mind, he withdrew into himself as a tortoise withdraws into its shell. This helped the BJP demonize the community.

The Bitter Truth

The Muslim attitude is not a political but a national problem. We did not do enough after 1947 to rehabilitate them in the national mainstream. The non-Muslim has always had it deeply embedded in his mind that Muslims are bigots, fanatics and treacherous. We were brought up on tales of heroism of Prithviraj Chauhan, Maharana Pratap, Guru Gobind Singh and Chhatrapati Shivaji. All our heroes were non-Muslims who had fought Muslims. Not one in our pantheon was Muslim. Akbar was just a token figure. We were exposed to evidence of what Muslim conquerors had done: desecrated our temples, massacred our citizenry and imposed humiliating taxes on them. Although all this ended with British rule, we continued to harbour distrust against Muslims. The more liberal kept up a facade of friendship with some, but rarely did we learn to relax in their company and speak our minds. They were not a part of the Indian mainstream. Jinnah did not have to invent the two-nation theory; it was there for anyone who had eyes to see. The British were quick to notice the distance between the communities, and as any other foreign power would have done, exploited it to their own advantage.

The Sangh and the BJP have capitalized on these old prejudices about Muslims. Ironically, these so-called nationalists in saffron have been doing exactly what the British did to rule over us. They will do everything in their power to keep the Muslims in ghettos, so that they remain the 'other'. This makes it easier for the Hindu fundamentalists to sell their lies to us. They tell us that the polygamous Muslims are multiplying at an alarming rate and soon Hindus will become a minority. We believe them, though census results clearly show that the rate of growth of the Hindu population has always been higher. They tell us that all Muslim rulers followed a policy of genocide against their Hindu subjects, when it is a proven fact of history that in India more Muslim blood was shed by Muslims than by Hindus. They tell us that today's Muslims resent not being the rulers of India and are intolerant and prone to violence. The fact is that in almost every communal confrontation since Independence, Muslim loss of life and property has been almost ten times that of the Hindus.

The BJP has succeeded in convincing many Hindus that Muslims were pampered and favoured throughout the time Congress was in power. I have already pointed out exactly what kind of pampering this was. To add to that argument I go back to Judge Madon's report, delivered after the Bhiwandi riots when the Congress was in power at the Centre and in Maharashtra. Although the Muslims were the victims (of the 121 killed, well over 100 were Muslims; of the property destroyed or looted, ninety per cent belonged to the

Muslims), the vast majority of those arrested were Muslims. The Maharashtra police disgraced their uniforms by showing pro-Hindu bias—they beat Muslim prisoners and deprived them of food and water (given to Hindu prisoners). The report also revealed that a Home Ministry circular giving instructions on how to deal with communal riots assumed, as do most non-Muslims, that it was the Muslims who created communal tensions. They were the ones to be watched.

The Hindu right has also targeted the Christians. Their numbers too, we are told, are increasing exponentially because of conversions. Many of us assume this is true. Find out for yourselves—the Christian population in India has in fact gone down. And why don't the Sanghwalas acknowledge that the missionaries have done more good for the country than they ever will? Christian missionaries did not limit themselves to preaching but put their beliefs into practice by opening schools, colleges and hospitals all over the country that are among the very best in India. In every natural calamity that visits our country, Christian relief workers are usually the first to arrive on the scene to the aid of the stricken. Everywhere they work among the sick and the diseased whom our society discards.

It is being insinuated that Christian institutions increased their activities encouraged by the fact that Sonia Gandhi, who has emerged as a contender for power, is a Catholic. This is absolute rubbish. Ever since she married Rajiv, she threw in her lot with her husband's community and besides paying homage to Mother Teresa, as millions of non-Christians did, kept aloof from religious organizations. She chose India as her home and brought up her children as Hindus though she had every right to bring them up as Christians.

Similar fancies and false arguments have been spread by the likes of Arun Shourie and Praful Goradia in their books and columns. They are intelligent, well read men. If they give us selective information and plain lies instead of proven facts, they do so with a purpose. Whipping up hatred among the majority community, emphasizing differences and creating grievances will win them elections.

Arthur Koestler in his *Suicide of a Nation* summed it up beautifully: 'Throughout the ages, painters and writers of fantastic tales have been fond of creating chimaeras (a monster with a lion's head, goat's torso and a serpent's tail). My own favourite brain-child is the momiphant. He is a phenomenon most of us have met in life: a hybrid who combines the delicate frailness of the Mimosa, crumbling at a touch when his own feelings are hurt, with the thick-skinned robustness of the elephant trampling over the feelings of others.' To me the Shouries and Goradias are classic momiphants. They will ruin the country.

We have helped them by not confronting our long history of prejudice. Every Indian community has kept itself apart from the others. It is time for us to accept this fact. The traditional approach to defuse communal tension was the Ram-Rahim or the Ishwar-Allah *teyro naam* approach, preaching that all religions emphasize love between humans. It worked when we had people like Mahatma Gandhi around because he symbolized in his own person the spirit of Allah and Ishwar. It works no more. C. Rajagopalachari used to say that God was our best policeman. It is true that a truly religious man has no hatred in him. But such men have become a rarity while those who display their religiosity by emphasizing differences between religions have become a common phenomenon. Most of us have double standards of judgement: we are unable to see the shortcomings of our own religions but more than eager to see the fatuous in other people's faiths. The Ram-Rahim approach is just a smoke screen.

Once we have seen the villain in ourselves, we will have taken the first step towards securing our future.

IS THERE A SOLUTION?

As our numbers multiply, so do our problems. I am convinced that the suicidal rate of increase of our population has contributed to the rising communal tension in our country. There is terrible congestion in our cities and small towns, where millions live cheek-by-jowl in filthy and trying conditions. Resources are scarce and there aren't enough jobs available. Naturally, tensions build up at the slightest provocation. Tempers are frayed and explode into violence. Instead of going for the person against whom you have a grievance, it is easier to gang up with members of your own community and go for those who are not.

Communal groups, of every community, have always taken advantage of this. The difference now is that Hindu communal groups are trying to unite the Hindus—eighty-two per cent of the population but traditionally divided into several mutually antagonistic caste and linguistic groups—to gang up against a common enemy. This common enemy according to them is the 'foreigner', namely the Muslims and the Christians who must be forced into a subordinate status or hounded out or even decimated.

In Gujarat we saw how the Sangh used the grievances of the poor and the jobless and the perpetually insecure and acquisitive Indian middle class to further its evil agenda.

Economic motives for violence have always been around and the minorities have always been the victims of such violence. The Moradabad riots were triggered by Punjabi immigrants wanting to break the Muslim monopoly over the brassware industry. It was the same in Jalgaon and Bhiwandi (Maharashtra) where outsiders, largely Sindhi and Punjabi Hindus, destroyed Muslim weavers in order to grab their business. In Haryana the Hindu backlash against Sikh terrorism in Punjab was directed against the Sikh shopkeepers of Panipat, Karnal and Yamunanagar. In riot-prone Hyderabad, Hindu mobs went for Muslim property including a Khadi Bhandar because the owner of the building was a Muslim. In Gujarat, not surprisingly, factories and shops owned by Muslims were burnt down, and in the villages, adivasis were let loose on Muslim money lenders.

A factor that adds to the problem is the rapidly increasing number of the educated unemployed. They were the single largest group behind terrorism in Punjab. It is the same in Kashmir. In Gujarat many of the Hindu terrorists who killed and raped Indian citizens were also unemployed men. Looting banks, robbing the rich, spreading terror gives them a sense of power.

The scenario is grim and getting grimmer day by day. What can be done about it?

First, we have to learn to live with it. As I have said before, we cannot wish communalism away. We cannot pretend communal differences are seen only during riots and don't exist otherwise. They always have and they will in the future. So we must all, Hindus, Muslims, Christians, Sikhs, somehow overcome our stereotyped notions of communities other than our own. We must avoid the tendency to build community-based housing societies, schools and clubs. Hindus and Sikhs must understand that the Muslims of India do not have to atone in perpetuity for the historical mistakes of some past rulers of their faith who were in fact more concerned about the security of their empires, not their religion. Muslims have as much right to this country as anyone else. If they are foreigners, we all are. The only people who are indigenous are the adivasis, whom we have all but made extinct.

The misuse of official media, All India Radio and Doordarshan, for propagating religion must stop. It has done immense harm by isolating communities further and putting the clock of scientific progress backwards. I attribute much of the blame for the resurgence of Hindu fundamentalism to serials on the *Ramayana* and the *Mahabharata*. The practice of religion must be restricted to places of worship and not imposed on others through public broadcasting means, loudspeakers, processions and holding samagams in public parks.

When we are face to face with communal passions, what are the preventive and punitive methods we should adopt? The most important preventive method is to strengthen our Intelligence. This has become a cliché but it is very important. Our Intelligence has been so poor that we hardly get a warning ahead of time that communal passions are building up. It is only after somebody has been stabbed or some houses burnt down that the police, as our newspapers say, swing into action.

We must also restructure our police force. We should adopt the simple principle that the minority communities should be over-represented. If it is a Muslim area the police should be largely Hindu. If it is a Hindu area the police should be largely Muslim. This is necessary because it restores confidence in the minorities as it is the fears of the minority that you have to try and assuage. Care should be taken to see that sub-inspectors certainly belong to minority communities because they are the most important police officers who deal with the actual situation in any particular area.

When a riot really breaks out, what should we do? I have the following suggestions to make:

First, wherever a riot breaks out, the police officer in charge should automatically be suspended, because the breakdown of the law enforcing machinery is clear evidence of dereliction of duty; it is the police officer's duty to know that tension was building up and he should have taken steps to defuse it. After a new police officer—preferably from outside the area—is put in charge, the entire administration of that particular locality should be placed in his or her hands. It is for the officer, along with the district magistrate, to impose curfew in the area and take whatever steps they want, to contain violence.

We must also provide for summary trials of mischief-makers. Perpetrators of communal riots are seldom brought to court. Rarely are communal killers punished, because nobody is willing to give evidence against them. Provisions should be made for summary trials on the spot where the incidents have taken place, and the magistrate should be empowered to impose collective fines on the area and to order public flogging of the people he feels were responsible.

Of course, none of this will work unless we unequivocally embrace the idea of secularism as defined in our Constitution and kick out any government that is even remotely communal. Otherwise we will have more governments like Modi's which will transfer out police officers not for their failure to prevent riots but for their failure to engineer and encourage them. It is tragic that we have corrupted the meaning of secularism, given it alternative definitions that suit us. Some people have even suggested we should banish secularism from India. Some five years ago, speaking at an official welcome function organized by the then BJP government of Delhi, the Shankaracharya said that the word 'secular' should be expunged from the Constitution. He need not have laboured the point: for all practical purposes, barring the communists most of our political leaders have deleted secularism from their lexicons. The Lakshman Rekha between politics and religion no longer exists. Religion has invaded the domain of politics and completely swamped it. Thus we have driven the last nail in the coffin of secularism as envisaged by Pandit Nehru.

At the cost of repetition, let me refresh readers' minds that secularism has two meanings: the Western concept makes a clear distinction between functions of the State which includes politics and functions of religion which are confined to places of worship, public or private. This is the concept that Nehru accepted, preached and practised. The other concept was equal respect for all religions. This was propagated and observed by men like Bapu

Gandhi and Maulana Azad and lasted as long as the two men were alive. After that it deteriorated to a mere display of religiosity. If you were a devout Hindu you went to a Muslim dargah or threw an Iftar party to prove you were secular. If you were Muslim, you celebrated Diwali with your Hindu friends. Secularism was reduced to a sham display. Time has shown that as far as secularism is concerned, Nehru was right; Gandhi and Azad were wrong.

The need of our times is to revive the Nehruvian notion of secularism. People in politics or holding elected public offices must not publicly engage themselves in religious rituals. Nehru never did. He did not encourage godmen, sants or mullahs or priests, to intrude into affairs of the State. The slide began with his daughter Indira Gandhi. With her, people like Dhirendra Brahmachari became formidable figures. Astrologers and tantrics were included in decision-making circles. We had the likes of Buta Singh, Balram Jakhar and Rajiv Gandhi paying homage to Deoraha Baba. We had the likes of Chandraswamy and Satellite Baba performing yagnas in homes of ministers and chief ministers. The Congress even wooed the Shahi Imam for the Muslim vote. And then we had Sahib Singh Verma's Delhi government and later the BJP-led NDA government inviting the Shankaracharya to be a State guest and to decide on legal issues of national import.

Religion is being brought into every aspect of life. This must stop; it is the road to madness. Sing your bhajans and shabads, say your namaaz and prayers as many times as you want, but in your home or your place of worship. That is for the salvation of your soul. Leave the soul of the nation to our Constitution and the law.

India Needs a New Religion

The ideal solution of course is for India to adopt a new religion. I know I am being unrealistic, but I would like to share this idea with my readers anyway. Perhaps a few of you will become converts to good sense and I will have done my bit to beat the 'fundoos'.

Bernard Shaw once wrote that every intelligent man makes his own religion though there are a hundred versions of it. Evolving a personal religion for myself has been a lifelong quest. It was, as Allama Iqbal put it:

> *Dhoondta phirta hoon main, ai Iqbal,*
> *apney aap ko*
> *Aap hee goya musafir, aap hee manzil*
> *hoon main*

> (O Iqbal, I go about everywhere looking for myself,

As if I were the wayfarer as well as
the destination)

After many years of the study of the religion
I was born into (Sikhism), studying the
scriptures and lives of founders of other major
religions of the world, and teaching
comparative religions at American universities,
I feel I am equipped to express myself on the
need to evolve a new religion for Indians who
have the courage to think for themselves. It is
based on the assumption that most people
need some kind of faith; that one's emotional
content is provided by the faith one is born
into, the rituals of which formed an essential
part of one's upbringing. What is required
today is the acceptance of what is basic in the
religion of birth but removing from it the
accretions of dead wood that have accumulated
around it and which militate against reason

and common sense. I present this for consideration and comment to my more enlightened countrymen.

I will first deal with five topics which are commonly regarded as the pillars of all religions: belief in God; reverence for avatars, prophets, messiahs and gurus who founded different religions; the place and use of religious scriptures; sanctity accorded to places for pilgrimage and worship; and the use of prayer and religious ritual. Since most of what I have to say on these topics may appear negatively critical, I will thereafter posit some items for positive acceptance.

*

Every religion has its own concept and name for God. What all of them have in common are God's attributes. God is the creator, preserver and destroyer; He is omniscient (all knowing) and omnipotent (all powerful); He is just and benign but can also be wrathful against transgressors. When pondering over the concept of God we have to answer the questions that Adi Shankara posed to himself over a thousand years ago:

Kustwam? ko ham? kutah ayatah?

Ko mein janani? ko mein tatah?

(Who am I? Where did I come from and how? Who are my real father and mother?)

The basic questions which beg for answers are, where do we come from? Why? Where do we go when we die?

Different religions give different answers to these questions. The answers can be grouped into two: those given by the Judaic family of religions (Judaism, Christianity and Islam) and those given by the Hindu family of religions (Hinduism, Jainism, Buddhism and Sikhism). The Judaic group will tell you that God created the world, sent Adam and Eve to propagate the human race and all other forms of life. According to this group, one day all life will end, there will be a day of judgement when people will rise from their graves to be judged for the good or evil they did in the world and be sent to heaven or hell accordingly. The Judaic-Christian-Muslim view of life is linear: it has a beginning, a middle and an end. According to the Hindu cyclical theory there is no beginning or end but a continuous unending cycle (samsara) of births, deaths and rebirths. There is no heaven or hell but reward or punishment in the form in which a person will be reborn. Its equivalent of heaven is release from samsara and union (yoga) with the divine. This is moksha, salvation.

However more complex or sophisticated the Hindu theory of samsara may appear when compared with the simplistic Judaic theory, there is as little evidence to support it as there is about Adam, Eve and the day of judgement. The stories of children remembering their earlier lives are figments of childish fantasy and largely confined to the Hindu family of religions. Every single case of parapsychology investigated by scientists has been found to be fraudulent. The simple truth is that we do not know where we come from and whether or not there is a divine purpose in our existence; we do not know where we go when we die. This is summed up beautifully in a couplet by Shaad Azimabadi:

Sunee hikayat-e-hastee to darmiyaan
  say sunee

Na ibtida kee khabar hai, noa intiha
  maaloom.

(All we've heard of the story of life is
  its middle.

We know not its beginning, we know
  not its end.)

Voltaire argued correctly when he said that he could scarcely believe that if there is a watch, there was no watchmaker. He went on to add 'If there were no God, it would be necessary to invent one.' Search for God is a quest in futility. 'Dare I say it?' asked Joubert, 'God may be easily known, only if it is not necessary to define him.' Once again the sense of frustration is aptly put in Urdu verse:

*Koee milney ko tera nishaan bhee
hai?*

*Koee rehney ka tera makaan bhee
hai?*

*Tera charcha jahaan kee zabaano peh
hai,*

*Tera shore zamaney kay kaanon mein
hai;*

*Magar aankhon say deykha to parda
hasheen,*

*Kaheen too na mila, tera ghar no
mila.*

(Is there an address where I can find
you?

Any home in which you reside?

Your name is on everyone's tongue,

Your fame rings in the world's ears;

But when I look for you, you are hid
behind a veil

I sought you everywhere but did not
find your abode.)

Aptly summing up the fruitless quest is another
couplet:

*Too dil mein to aataa hai, samajh
mein nahin aataa,*

*Bus jaan gaya ke teri pahchan yahee
hai.*

(You come into my heart but I cannot
understand you.

It's enough that I know this is the
only way to know you.)

We are on trickier ground when we describe
God as omniscient, omnipotent, benign and
just. There is so much injustice in the world,
so much suffering imposed on the innocent
and the god-fearing that it can scarcely be

argued that there is a divine purpose behind it. When a child of seven going to school is crushed to death by a drunk truck driver who gets away with it, how can anyone ascribe it to a merciful and just God? Either He did not have the power to prevent the accident or was callous enough to inflict suffering on the child's family. Where was God when evil-minded people planted a bomb in the Kanishka and sent hundreds of innocent men, women and children to a watery grave? Or when an earthquake destroys an entire village? Unless we can answer these questions rationally and not shelter behind explanations like 'atoning for sins committed in previous births' or being rewarded in heaven, it is better to keep silent.

It is best to accept Darwin's theory of the origins of life on earth. At least it takes us back to the amoeba. Not even scientists are able to discover who created the amoeba, the sun, the moon and the galaxy of stars. Neither have scientists or spiritualists yet been able to probe beyond the mysteries of death or evidence of a life hereafter. Under the circumstances the only honest answer an intelligent person can give to the question 'Is there a God?' is to say, 'I do not know.'

The important thing to remember is that belief in God has nothing to do with being good or bad. You can be a saintly person without believing in God and a detestable villain believing in Him. In my religion God has no place.

*

In every religion the founder is more revered than God for the simple reason that people know a little more about their prophets, avatars, messiahs or gurus than they know about God. They were human beings with superhuman powers with which they were able to sway the masses. Inevitably, with the passage of years, their admirers created so many legends about them that they ceased to be human! They became reincarnations of God, His progeny, His specially chosen messengers, and invariably with direct access to Him. The truth of the matter is that we have hardly any hard, reliable evidence on what kind of human beings they were. In dehumanizing them, we have done them injustice, making them incomparably good and therefore beyond human striving. We can see the process of deification taking place in the Indians' perception of Mahatma Gandhi. Here we had as great a man as any the world has seen, but also full of human frailties. Not one of his four sons got on with him; one even embraced Islam to spite him. He was vain, took offence at the slightest remark against him, and a fad-ist who made nubile girls lie naked next to him to make sure that he had overcome his libidinous desires. All these failings which make him human and down to earth and yet hold him up as a shining example of a human being for all of mankind are being lost thanks to our putting him on a pedestal and worshipping him. It is time we learnt to give avatars and prophets their proper places as important historical personalities who did good to humanity. No more than that.

*

All religious scriptures are held in awe either as words of God or divinely inspired utterances. I have read all of them, many times. Without exception they are unscientific (one can't blame their authors as at the time science was little advanced), repetitive and tediously boring. Those that enshrined codes of conduct and ethics undoubtedly served a useful purpose and many passages have a literary quality. I often quote the Bible, the Koran, the Upanishads and the Granth Sahib. These are works of literature that cannot be compared with the great classics of Kalidas, Shakespeare, Goethe, Tolstoy, Ghalib, Tagore or Iqbal.

However, this is my personal view of holy texts and is not shared by anyone I have met. Most people are deeply moved by scriptural revelations. So who am I to tell them that their response is conditioned by continuous indoctrination? But they cannot fault me when I maintain that scriptures for whatever they are worth should be read and understood and not worshipped. In this context the most difficult phenomenon to explain is the way Sikhs, who others boast of not being idol worshippers, treat their sacred book. They put it to bed at night, rouse it in the morning, drape it in expensive raiment, have elaborate canopies over it, wave fly whisks while reading it, take it out in massive processions. They organize non-stop readings of it (akhand path) that last for two days and nights by a relay of readers (often hired at different rates for different purposes), and believe that its recitation, even when they are asleep in another room, does them good. I often wonder what the gurus whose works are compiled in the Granth Sahib would have had to say of their followers, few of whom even try to understand their message.

*

I believe that the only legitimate place of worship is the home. However, there are religions like Islam which emphasize congregational namaaz in a public mosque as a religious obligation; Christianity which enjoins attendance at masses; there are temples and gurudwaras without which kirtans and kathas (sermons) would lose their impact. In a country which has few diversions like clubs, pubs and picture houses, places of worship provide free, harmless entertainment and the company of like-minded people. But in recent years, places of worship have been turned into arenas of contention and have been misused to propagate ideas other than those religious. Some years ago the Kaaba was the scene of a pitched battle; the Golden Temple, particularly the Akal Takht, had been under the control of gun-toting men spouting hate rather than spreading the message of love that their gurus preached. And of course there has been plenty of bad blood over the Ramjanmabhoomi-Babri Masjid dispute. The government should, as a matter of policy, forbid the building of any more places of worship. We have more than enough of them. The government should never permit the use of public parks or open spaces for religious gathering, and if a place of worship becomes a bone of contention or happens to be misused by undesirable elements, it should simply take it over.

A Punjabi Sufi poet reflects my sentiments on the subject:

> *Masjid dhaa dey, mandir dhaa dey,*
> *dhaa dey jo kuchh dhainda:*
> *Ikk kisay da dil na dhaaven,*
> *Rab dilaan vicch rehnda.*

> (Break the mosque, break the temple,
> break whatever besides;

But break not a human heart because

that's where God resides.)

*

It cannot be disputed that we Indians, whether we be Hindus, Muslims, Christians, Sikhs or Parsees, spend more time on religious ritual than any other people in the world. The Hindi adage 'saat vaar aur aath teohaar (there are seven days in the week but eight religious festivals)' is not an overstatement. Count the number of religious holidays we have in a year. Then add up the number of hours people spend saying their prayers, going to places of worship, on pilgrimages, attending satsangs, listening to pravachans, kirtans, bhajans, qawwalis etc. It comes to a staggering total. Ask yourself if a developing nation like India can afford to expend so much time in pursuits that produce no material benefits. Also ask yourself, does strict adherence to the routine of prayer or telling beads of the rosary make someone a better person? Is it not true that even dacoits pray for the success of their mission before they set out on it, and that the worst black marketers and tax evaders are often very devout?

Agreed that it is entirely up to all individuals to spend his or her time as they like. If they get fulfilment out of prayer and ritual they have every right to do so. But what men of religion have no right to do is to impose their religiosity on other people. The use of loudspeakers for azaan or kirtan and bhajan mandalis amounts to such an imposition. The craziest example is the all-night jagarans which disturb the sleep of entire localities. The use of official media like radio and TV for propagating religions through broadcasts of celebrations and hymns needs to be curbed. Taking out processions through crowded bazaars and upsetting civic life also amounts to imposition of one's ritual on other people, and should be discouraged.

A modern fad which has gained widespread acceptance amongst the semi-educated who wish to appear secular is the practice of meditation. They proclaim with an air of smug superiority, 'Main mandir-vandir nahin jaata, meditate karta hoon (I don't go to temples or other such places, I meditate).' The exercise involves sitting lotus-pose (padma asana), regulating one's breathing and making your mind go blank to prevent it from 'jumping about like monkeys' from one (thought) branch to another. This intense concentration awakens the kundalini serpent coiled at the base of the spine. It travels upwards through chakras (circles) till it reaches its destination in the cranium. Then the kundalini is fully jaagrit (roused) and the person is assured to have reached his goal. What does meditation achieve? The usual answer is 'peace of mind'. If you probe further, 'and what does peace of mind achieve?', you will get no answer because there is none. Peace of mind is a sterile concept which achieves nothing. The exercise may be justified as therapy for those with disturbed minds or those suffering from hypertension, but there is no evidence to prove that it enhances creativity. On the contrary it can be established by statistical data that all the great works of art, literature, science and music were works of highly agitated minds, at times minds on the verge of collapse. Allama Iqbal's short prayer is pertinent:

Khuda tujhey kisee toofaan say aashna
kar dey

Keh terey beher kee maujon mein
iztiraab naheen

(May God bring a storm in your life,
There is no agitation in the waves of
your life's ocean.)

A word which constantly appears in the Allama's writings is 'talaatum', restlessness of the mind, as the sine qua non of creativity.

The new religion of India should be based on a work ethic. It should provide leisure time to recoup one's energy to resume work, but discourage uncreative pastimes. We must not waste time. There is a hadith of the Prophet which says:

La tasabuddhara Innadhawa;

Hoo Wallahoo.

(Don't waste time; time is God.)

*

I would like to sum up all that I have said about prayer, ritual and meditation in a slogan I have coined as a motto for modern India: 'Work is worship, but worship is not work.'

I believe that the essence of every person's religion should be the endeavour not to hurt another person or living thing and to preserve his environment. Ahimsa Paramo Dharma— nonviolence is the supreme religion. Nonviolence in this context is not a negative but a positive concept, requiring promotion of goodwill and preservation of life. Violence is the ultimate form of vulgarity and has to be eschewed in action and in speech.

Our religion should make provision for the future. It should incorporate family planning. After the birth of two children, parents should be required to undergo sterilization. We have no right to overload an already over-populated country. Likewise cutting down trees, polluting catchment areas, rivers, lakes and seas should be regarded as irreligious acts. The earth is also in dire need of rejuvenation. We are fast denuding it of its forest cover and making it sterile by using of chemical fertilizers, and destroying bird and insect life through the use of insecticides. Humans when they die should be returned to the earth from which, according to most religions, they emanate. Destruction of forests to provide wood for construction must be stopped forthwith. Where gas or electric crematoriums are not available, the dead, irrespective of their religion, should be buried, not in permanent graves which render land unproductive, but in open spaces earmarked for the purpose. And every third year the ground should be tilled and returned to agricultural use.

I will sum up my faith in time-worn cliches: good life is the only religion. Ingersoll put it in more felicitous language: 'Happiness is the only good; the place to be happy is here; the time to be happy is now; the way to be happy is to help others.' Ella Wheeler Wilcox put the same thought in plainer words:

> 'So many gods, so many creeds, so many paths that wind and wind
>
> When just the art of being kind is all that the sad world needs.'